The Brightest Bulb

Written by
Vanessa Cain

To Loki, the brightest bulb in our family.

To Nancy, Richard, and Tanya Jackson – **Go Team!**
To Tanya Foster and Julie Smith, for being my truth-tellers, and hug givers.
To Danielle, Jazzmin, Joseph, Makenzie, and Alora – my babies.
Most of all, **to my son Tyler**, for being my reason for everything!

Published in association with
Bear With Us Productions

© 2021 Vanessa Cain
The Brightest Bulb

The right of Vanessa Cain as the author of this work has been asserted by her in accordance with the Copyright Designs and Patents Act 1988.
All rights reserved, including the right of reproduction in whole or part in any form.

ISBN: 978-1-7370087-0-5

Cover by Richie Evans
Design by Luisa Moschetti
Illustrated by Caner Soylu

www.justbearwithus.com

Illustrated by
Caner Soylu

The Brightest Bulb

Written by
Vanessa Cain

Once there was a Christmas Bulb.
He was not very bright.

Other bulbs would laugh at him
And say he was a sight.

Still, Little Bulb tried his best.
He wanted to fit in,

But no matter how he tried
He was just a bit too dim.

He was never good at school.
Teachers called him lazy.

Some called him a nerdy bulb,
Others said, "He's crazy."

Bulb had a strange desire.
To him, the idea was scary,

But if he could find a job
His Christmas would be Merry.

Bob was good at his job,
No problem was too large.

He could find a place for Bulb
Because he was *Head Elf In Charge.*

Bob sent Little Bulb to try out jobs.
He was curious to see which would fit.

Little Bulb worked hard and tried them all,
It was not in him to quit.

He wanted to help with the caroling.
He thought he could sing of things merry,

But alas Little Bulb was horrible
And the notes he couldn't carry.

He wanted to try out baking
Candies, cookies, and all things good.

The Pastry Elf tried his cake and said, "Goodness, it takes like wood."

Next he tried helping at the stables
For he loved to play with the reindeer.

Yet again Little Bulb was rejected
And told, "Sorry you can't remain here."

Bob saw what a hard time Bulb was having
And said, "Maybe letters are your thing?"

But the Postmaster Elf said Bulb was too slow
And cried, "With his help, we'll be here till Spring."

Little Bulb could not find a job,
He was drowning in defeat.

But Bob told Bulb, "Until you find work,
my job is not complete."

Bob bowed his head and frowning said,
"Don't let trying make you blue."

"You will find work my little friend. I wouldn't say it if it were not true."

Encouraged, Little Bulb lifted his chin.
It was out there if he just kept looking.

He would find a way to make Christmas,
Just nothing with singing, animals, or cooking.

Then Little Bulb showed up at the Workshop.
He begged them just to let him stay,

But with no skills to paint, wrap, or hammer,
They simply had to send him away.

One day he came upon the town square
With everyone near a huge tree.

They were coming together to decorate,
And Little Bulb's heart filled with glee.

Ribbons came forward and other bulbs too,
On branches and boughs they did sit,

But when Little Bulb tried to get on the tree
They said, "Surely you don't think you fit?"

Little Bulb hung his head in shame.
How was he expected to cope?

Bulb had failed at every job,
He had no reason to hope.

Then Santa called out to him,
"Buddy, aren't you having any fun?"

Bulb looked at Santa embarrassed,
Now he just wanted to run.

Having no job in front of Santa,
The very thought of it was grim.

"Why look so low, little guy?"
Bulb answered, "Santa, I-I'm just too dim."

"I see there's a spot right under the star,
and I think that would suit you just fine."

But Bulb bowed his head and sadly replied,
"The brightest light on that tree won't be mine."

"You're right," said Santa, "But look again. Don't you see what has begun?"

"No one is worried about the job they have. They're all just having fun."

"No one cares who made the cookies,
or if the cocoa gets reheated."

"To make Christmas happy, the only real truth,
Is that every Bulb is needed."

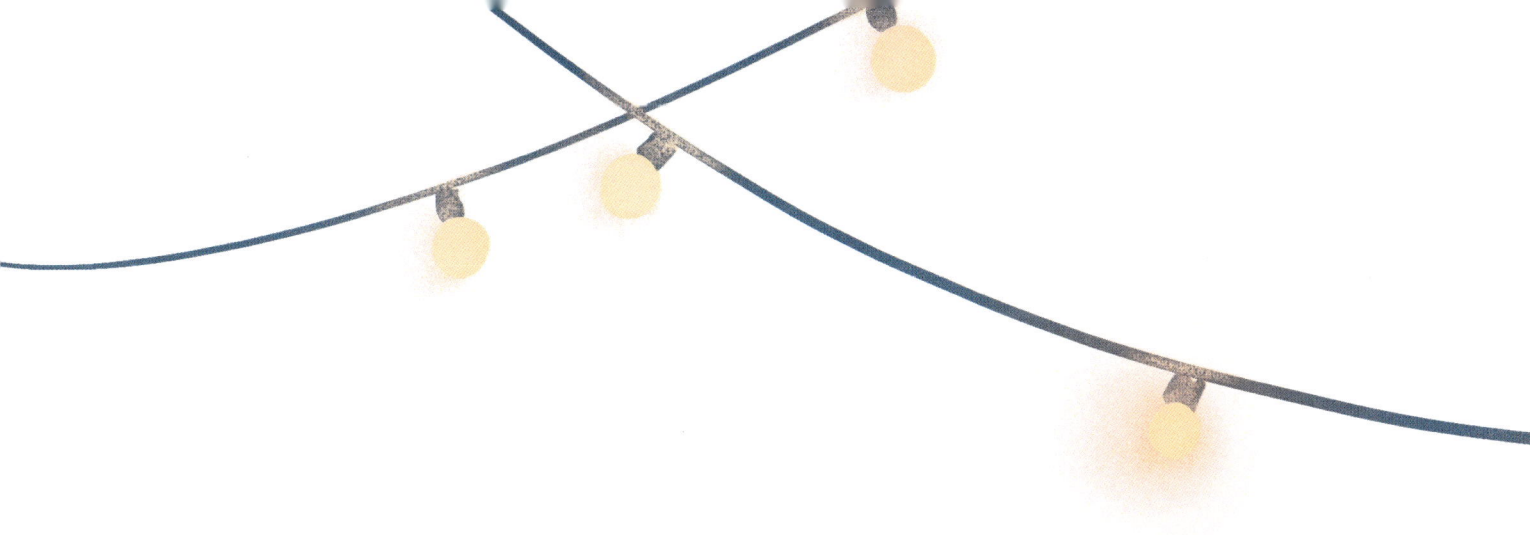

Then Santa bent and lifted Little Bulb to his spot.
"You look good sitting there on that tree."

"And if anyone doubts your position or place,
My friend, they will answer to me."

Bulb couldn't believe it. It felt like a dream.
The bough under the star was so fine,

But he took a deep breath, blew out his cheeks,
And Little Bulb started to shine.

Everyone cheered, even the reindeer smiled.
"That a boy," said Bob, the Head Elf.

About the author

Vanessa Cain is a lover of books.
She is an avid reader, and has been writing since the age of 8, when she was gifted her first journal.
Though this is her first foray into writing children's literature, Vanessa is a storyteller.
Through her poetry, playwrighting, and other fiction, she loves to create ways for people to connect, or get lost for a little while in the lines she writes.

Vanessa is a consummate student.
She is passionate about Child Evangelism, TEFL, interfaith initiatives, and stories with uniquely flawed characters. Through her ministry and evangelism work, Vanessa aims to encourage people, especially children, to know their worth in spite of any perceived flaws or failings.

Visit the author's website at www.vanessacainwrites.com
Or email her directly at author@vanessacainwrites.com

Made in the USA
Middletown, DE
03 November 2021